HISTORIC ASHCROFT

ASHCROFT

FOR THE STRONG EYE ONLY

HISTORIC ASHCROFT:
FOR THE STRONG EYE ONLY

PAT FOSTER

PLATEAU PRESS
KAMLOOPS, BRITISH COLUMBIA

Plateau Press
PO Box 283
Kamloops, BC
V2C 5K6
Fax (250) 314-1803

Canadian Cataloguing in Publication Data

Foster, Pat, 1929
  Historic Ashcroft

  Includes bibliographical references
  ISBN 0-9698842-3-0

  1. Ashcroft (B.C.)--History. I. Title.
FC3849.A85F67 1999   971.1'72   C99-910247-8
F1089.5.A79F67 1999

Cover photograph from BCARS D-09299

Printed in Canada by Navigator Communications

Plateau Press is distributed by: Sandhill Book Marketing,
                                   99-1270 Ellis Street,
                                   Kelowna, BC
                                   V1Y 1Z4
                                   Telephone (250) 763-1406
                                   Fax (250) 763-4051

Contents

JUST A PIECE OF BROWN PAPER

Despite its unique desert setting in the beautiful valley of the Thompson River, the landscape and climate of Ashcroft don't appeal to everyone. As Bruce Hutchison says in his well known book *The Fraser* (where he manages to discuss the Thompson River as well): "The scenery from Ashcroft is for the strong eye only." And he was just passing through! Many years after she and her family arrived here, Dorothy Goldrick still recalled her first reaction: "I remember how devastating it seemed to come from England's green and pleasant land to Ashcroft, because it was sand hills, sagebrush, tumbleweed and a few rattlers here and there. And the heat! Old Doctor Sanson used to say there was only just a piece of brown paper between Ashcroft and hell."

True, Ashcroft does not have the lush green charm of Vancouver Island, nor the lofty grandeur of the Rocky Mountains, and, yes, there is an abundance of sand hills, sagebrush and tumbleweed. One does still see the occasional rattlesnake. Nevertheless, there is a remarkable beauty here that changes constantly and repays the perceptive observer with breathtaking diversity.

It does get very hot in Ashcroft, but only for a few weeks in mid-summer and, even then, it is not even close to hell. The climate is quite moderate most of the year, and it is a gardener's delight thanks to the abundance of water from the Thompson River. As travellers come down the long hill into town from either direction, they are amazed by this oasis in the desert—the lush green of the trees and lawns, the incredible growth of the gardens, especially tomatoes and potatoes, for which the area is justly famous.

The region attracted settlers who were hard working, adventurous, and tenacious, who took time to care about their neighbours and enjoy a little fun in their spare time. You will still find the same kind of people here—self-sufficient, but warm and friendly folks who make you feel welcome. You are not a stranger for long.

The Ashcroft area has undergone many name changes over the years. It was called Tuk Tuk Chim by the local natives, Harper's Mill by the pioneers, St. Cloud by Van Horne of the CPR, Barnes Station by freighters and prospectors, and finally Ashcroft Station, which was shortened to Ashcroft by the Postal Service, much to the chagrin of Clement Cornwall. The Cornwalls had given the name Ashcroft to their ranch and roadhouse, about five miles from the present town site, after their original home in England, and they established the first Ashcroft Post Office there. C.F. Cornwall, in a letter to the *B.C. Mining Journal* in 1899, insisted vigorously that the name of the town should remain Ashcroft Station. He argued that Ashcroft was the name of his property and that it should exclusively remain so. Cornwall never agreed to the change.

With the arrival of the CPR in 1884, the completion of the bridge across the Thompson River in 1886, and the establishing of the BX Express headquarters here in 1887, Ashcroft became the new gateway to the Cariboo. The *B.C. Directory* of that year lists eighty buildings and a population of approximately one hundred in the little town. A period of growth and prosperity began, which lasted, with some ups and downs, until the completion of the Pacific Great Eastern Railway, which spelled the end of the glory days of the BX. This and the devastating fire of 1916 dealt a staggering blow to the economy of the town.

Vegetable farming, done mostly by the Chinese, provided a boost to the business community when Ashcroft became known as "Spud City" thanks to the quantity and high quality of the potatoes grown here. Helping Ashcroft weather the Great Depression was the commercial growing of tomatoes, starting in 1924. The old BX stable was converted into a cannery, which operated successfully until 1957 when it was closed. Local ranchers at that time wanted their land for more lucrative crops, and the younger Chinese workers moved to the lower mainland seeking better jobs or further education.

Copper mining in the Highland Valley increased the population for some years, but the construction of the Coquihalla Highway and the building of the instant town of Logan Lake caused many miners to leave Ashcroft. Many Greyhound employees also left at that time. Today, with the world price of copper remaining depressed, the closure of the mine is a real possibility--one that would hurt the local economy significantly.

Today, Ashcroft is becoming a new Mecca for retired people who love its climate, its comfortable, relaxed lifestyle, and down-home atmosphere. This book is written by one of these, a relative newcomer, who, without benefit of a "strong" eye, views the magnificent landscape and finds herself closer to heaven than to hell.

I am indebted to the British Columbia Archives and Records Service (BCARS) and the Ashcroft Museum for the photographs included in the book. I want to thank a few people in particular for their assistance in the preparation of this little book. However, a mere thank you to Helen Forster, Curator of the Ashcroft Museum and Archives, hardly seems sufficient for the invaluable advice she has given me in researching and in checking the manuscript for historical accuracy. I want to thank my husband, Norm Foster, whose advice on the "readability" of the book was so helpful, and Wayne Norton, who had the original idea for this project and encouraged my work on it.

FREIGHTING ALONG THE CARIBOO ROAD: CATALINE AND HIS PEERS

For many years freighters plied their trade along the Cariboo Road, moving huge quantities of supplies to those who lived and worked along its route. Originally they hauled from Yale to Barkerville, but after the CPR reached Ashcroft in 1884, the freighters loaded up here. The streets of Ashcroft were alive with freighters and their animals from 1886 until well after the turn of the century. The forwarding agents did a massive business bringing in hundreds of thousands of pounds of material by train, and dispatching it to outlying areas by the pack trains and freight wagons. For example, during one week in August 1895, 450,000 pounds of freight arrived by train in Ashcroft; by the next week it was in wagons on its way north. During that summer, the Whittler Concessions Company alone received 640,000 pounds of pipe and machinery. Other shipments included foodstuffs, building supplies, furniture—in fact, anything that the people and businesses saw fit to order.

During the 1890s, there were literally hundreds of covered wagons pulled by horse teams and oxen engaged in the freighting business. Ashcroft's Harvey Bailey Company alone had an average of seventy-five freight wagons, pulled by teams of six to twelve horses, constantly on the road, each hauling from 9,000 to 18,000 pounds of goods. Some single pieces of machinery weighed as much as 14,000 pounds. In addition, the company sent out large pack trains of mules, each animal carrying as much as 400 pounds, the whole train conveying goods weighing from 9,000 to 15,000 pounds.

In the early 1860s, freight rates were around $1 a pound, making the retail cost of goods in the Cariboo very high. For example, a pound of butter cost $5, a pound of flour $2. With the opening of the new road and the increase in the number of packers, these rates decreased steadily. According to the

Ashcroft Journal, by 1896 the cost of transporting a pound of freight from Ashcroft to 150 Mile house was 2 cents, to Horsefly 2 1/2 cents, Quesnelle 3 1/2 cents, and Barkerville 5 cents.

The earliest miners carried all their worldly possessions on their backs, walking the entire distance from Yale to the Cariboo gold fields, through the great variety of terrain covered by the Cariboo Trail—from dry belt to wetlands, from rugged mountains to rolling hills. One unique form of transportation used first by Andrew Olson was the trundle-barrow. In the early 1860s Olson, George Cook, and brothers William and Henry Downs built their own special version of the wheelbarrow, with its single wheel measuring four feet in diameter and with handles at both ends. It took two men to operate each barrow, the front man pulling and steering, and the rear man pushing or holding back as necessary, up hills, through streams and down steep grades. Each barrow could be loaded with up to four hundred pounds of food, clothing, seeds and tools. It was easier than packing supplies on their backs, but still required a great deal of strength and stamina.

Soon other modes of transportation were introduced, one of the most controversial being the camels introduced to the area in 1862 by Frank Laumeister, Henry Ingram and Adam Heffley. Since these animals had been used with some success in the desert of southwest United States, it seemed logical that they would do well in transporting goods in the BC interior. However, when they arrived in Victoria, the very sight of them according to one account frightened a native observer to death. They had a most disagreeable odour and an even worse disposition, and would attack any man or beast to whom they took a dislike, and these were many. Mules, oxen and horses along the Cariboo Road were spooked and took flight at the sight of a camel train. It is no wonder that there were protests against their use, petitions by other freighters to have them barred from the road, and threats of lawsuits. The camels' hoofs proved to be too soft for the rough terrain, and by 1864 Laumeister and his partners had given up the whole idea. They sold what few animals they could find buyers for, and turned the rest loose to forage for themselves on the meadows of the Upper Fraser-Thompson flats. The last one died in 1905, after forty-three years in this inhospitable land.

One of the earliest men in the transportation business was Frances James Barnard. Several times in 1864, from spring until early fall, he walked from Yale to the Cariboo gold fields carrying mail, newspapers and small parcels on his back for the small charge of $2 per letter, $1 per newspaper. The next year he was awarded the government postal contract and bought a small mule to carry the load. In 1863, when the road was completed to Soda Creek, Barnard bought a two-horse wagon to carry three passengers as well as the mail and freight, and in 1864 he put the first four-horse, fourteen-passenger stages on the road. Two years later, he bought out Dietz & Nelson of Victoria, gaining control of the express and passenger business from Victoria to all points in British Columbia, and in 1868 he added six-horse stages. By this time, his wagons and stages covered over 110,000 miles a year, carrying 1500 passengers annually, gold valued at well over $4 million, as well as hundreds of pieces of express.

Steve Tingley started his career with the BX in 1867 and progressed from driver to partner to sole owner by 1884. That year the CPR reached Ashcroft and in 1886, after a bridge was completed over the Thompson River linking the town to the Cariboo Road, Tingley moved the BX headquarters to Ashcroft. There it remained until 1920, when the advent of truck transport and the completion of PGE railroad caused the BX to go out of business.

The BX was the first land transportation system west of the Rockies, and eventually, with routes covering over a thousand miles, second in size only to the legendary Wells Fargo. It is interesting to note that although Governor Douglas, with the Royal Engineers at his disposal, would not guarantee safe delivery of gold from the Cariboo, the BX did. As it happened, there were surprisingly few robberies. There was one in 1886 by two hold-up men, but no arrest was ever made, and another in the late 1890s in which there was no trace of a hold-up man. (The driver who was alone at the time was suspected, but there was no proof.) A robbery in 1890 saw an elderly man named Rowlands caught and jailed; Harry Brown was sentenced to fifteen years in the penitentiary for another in 1894; a man and a woman were suspected in a 1909 hold-up, but there was insufficient evidence to prosecute.

A wagon pulled by a twelve-mule team brought in by a Mr. Bates in 1863 was the first of its kind ever used for freighting on the Cariboo Road. Many more were soon to follow. Freighters often favoured teams of oxen, since, although they were slow, they were very strong and steady. The "bull puncher" walked beside the animals, urging them on when necessary with a "goad stick" or a blacksnake (whip), and on a good day a team would travel about ten miles. It took over a month to make the trip from Yale to Barkerville, so only two or three trips in a year were possible. Horse teams pulling wagons could make the trip in two weeks, while the stage took four days. Ashcroft pioneer Bill Baker remembered that it took half a day for a freighter pulled by a bull team to get from Ashcroft up the long hill to Boston Flats, a distance of about three miles. The last load of freight up the Cariboo Road using oxen left Ashcroft in September 1899. I.W. Strout, one of the most notable of the bull punchers, was the driver of twenty-four oxen pulling three wagons on this historic occasion.

Often two or three wagons would be joined together, pulled by twelve horses or mules. Because reins were not practical, a jerk line was used. This was a long line connected to the harness of the lead horses. The driver, who either walked or rode on a board at the side of the front wagon, "telegraphed" directions with the jerk line to the well-trained leaders who would stop or turn left or right according to the number of jerks on the line.

There were hundreds of freighters on the road, men of all races and personalities, Europeans, Chinese, and native

Indians. Most of those who drove horse teams wore a kind of uniform consisting of a narrow-brimmed cowboy hat, well-fitting leather gloves, flat heeled cowboy boots with the tops under their pants and the pants rolled up one turn for each pair of horses in his team. Most of these men were single and were not at all inclined to turn into family men. Some slept in hotels when in Ashcroft or one of the larger towns, but many spent the nights in their wagon boxes or in the haylofts above where their horses were stabled for the night. On the road they slept under the stars.

A coach and six near Ashcroft, circa 1897
(Courtesy Ashcroft Museum)

New arrivals to this part of the country often worked as freighters for a few years until they had enough money to purchase a business or a ranch, but for some it was their life's work. Notable among the latter were Harry Stout, Sam McDonald and Jean Jacques Caux. Stout, one of the earliest and best known of the bull team drivers, worked on the road until about 1895. McDonald drove mule and ox teams from New Westminster through Yale to the Cariboo for many years, and one of his wagons is now prominently displayed in downtown Ashcroft. This wagon, built by I. Lehman in Yale and restored by R.D. Cumming in 1932, is said to be the oldest wagon of its kind still in existence. McDonald and his son William freighted together for several years, and they drove the first herd of horses to pass through the Crowsnest Pass to Calgary.

Among pack train operators, the man called Cataline was a genuinely unique character. He was born Jean Jacques Caux in 1830 at Oleron-Sainte Marie, in the mountainous Bearn region of France, near Catalonia in Spain, and hence his nickname. There has been speculation that difficulty with the government of Napoleon III forced him to make a speedy exit from his native land. In 1858 he arrived in British Columbia along with the hundreds of Americans and Europeans who had heard about the gold discovery in the Cariboo. Rather than join in the rush for gold, he bought a mule train, and started packing supplies to the rapidly developing mining areas.

Of medium height but powerfully built, Cataline was a match for any unruly animal or human he might run into, and when he was around a pack train there was no doubt about who was in charge. He ran an efficient business and made a good deal of money, which he spent liberally on himself and on others. Although he employed men of all nationalities, he preferred the thickset northern Chinese, whom he found to be the most reliable and hard working. He would tell anyone who cared to listen that white men only stayed until they found a promising site to dig for gold, and Indians left as soon as they got paid, but the Chinese stayed at the job until it was done.

Three Chinese were trusted employees of Cataline for many years: Ah Gun who acted as supercargo; "Pretty" who handled one of the pack trains while Cataline looked after the other; and Bing Lo, who, according to Charles Gordon, an old-timer of Ashcroft, kept his employer's books in Chinese. However, it is generally believed that Cataline, who was able only to sign his name (and that with difficulty) relied mainly on his phenomenal memory to keep track of his accounts. When it was time to pay his employees, he could tell them exactly how much they had earned, what they had received in advances or goods, and what was coming to them. Similarly, when he received a bill from a merchant he had to be told what it said, but then he could tell to the penny if it was correct or not. If his numbers did not agree with theirs, his usually proved to be correct.

Talking with him must have been an experience. He indiscriminately mixed English, Spanish, French, Chinese and Shuswap words in a lingo that was mind-boggling. Especially recalled was his spectacular profanity, which was invariably accompanied by equally spectacular gestures.

His appearance was as remarkable as his language. A Spanish style black hat with a very wide brim and colourful band around the crown sat atop his black hair which was squared off at the shoulder. Under his knee-length frock coat he had a white shirt (a new one every trip) to which he fastened a collar only on special occasions, and a wide red sash for a belt. Unlike the teamsters, he tucked his pants into his boots, which were made of the finest calfskin and in which he carried a long Mexican knife. Under no conditions did he ever wear socks or mitts or ear coverings. His saddle horses were equally impressive— handsome, well-bred animals, their saddles and bridles were of the finest leather lavishly trimmed with silver.

Cataline used Spanish aparejoes instead of the more usual packsaddle, and soon other packers were following his lead. An aparejoe was a leather pad stuffed with hay with a large basket attached on each side. When this was put on the back of the mule or pack horse, up to one hundred pounds more could be carried without undue stress on the animal because the weight was spread over a larger area.

He had regular stopping places along the Cariboo Road where there was grass for his mules. Every night the animals were unloaded and the packs arranged in a circle, the animals put out to pasture, and then the men ate their simple meals. Cataline's consisted mainly of bannock, beans, game when it was available, and raw herbs and weeds which he kept in vinegar. They slept outdoors, and in the morning prepared to reload the animals, each of which went directly to its own aparejoe and waited its turn to be loaded.

During the winter when travel to the gold fields was virtually impossible, he wintered his animals at Marble Canyon and in later years at Dog Creek where he made his headquarters.

Cataline prided himself on delivering such fragile items as panes of glass and a grand piano. However, there was one item entrusted to Cataline that was not delivered. A native packer noticed a terrible smell coming from a food parcel and thought it was rotten. "She smell like Hell so I throw him in the river," he said when questioned about the package after the pack train arrived in Barkerville. The customer was no doubt very disappointed that his several pounds of Limburger cheese were destroyed in transit.

There are many stories about this remarkable man. One says that a European nobleman once mistook him for the governor of the territory, possibly because of his clothing, and bought him a drink. When the European asked if he did indeed have the privilege of drinking with the governor, Cataline rather testily replied: "Catalonia, (one of his favourite expletives) no! Me, I work!"

Cataline counted among his friends men from all walks of life—the Chinese and native Indians who worked for him, miners whom he grubstaked, ranchers, merchants, and judges. He was a faithful friend. In an interview, Nellie Baker recalled going with her father Doc English to Cataline's cabin near the Cornwall's ranch at Ashcroft. "He was a great old friend. I thought he was the greatest old fellow. First time I tasted rum, old Cataline gave me a spoon and I cleaned out his cup. It was sugar and rum, you know."

The story goes that someone who was railing loudly against Judge Matthew Begbie's methods of administering justice turned to Cataline and demanded to know whose side he was on. Cataline pulled his knife (with which he was very skilful) out of his boot. "I stand by the judge," he roared and that ended the discussion. This paid a big dividend when Cataline wanted to pre-empt some land in the Cariboo, which he could not do legally because he had never got around to taking out citizenship. When Begbie found out about this, he arranged to meet Cataline on the Cariboo Trail, held court on the spot, and Cataline immediately became a naturalized Canadian and landowner.

Cataline enjoyed a long and healthy life, despite (or because of) his winter morning ritual of rushing outside naked and rubbing snow all over his body, and his liberal use of rum, both as a libation and as hair lotion. He was widely known and respected in his own time, and is still seen as the prototype of the colourful men who freighted on the Cariboo Trail. After gold became harder to find and Barkerville's prosperous days were over, Cataline, who was known by then as "King of the Packers," was still running his pack trains as far as Hazelton, serving the Hudson's Bay Company and the Yukon Telegraph maintenance men in that remote area. In 1913, after fifty-five years on the road, he retired in Hazelton, where he was no doubt the town character until his death in 1922.

For over sixty years, Cataline, Harry Stout, Sam McDonald, Bill Bose and other freighters kept the lifeline to the Cariboo and Chilcotin open, allowing the miners, ranchers and businessmen to develop the central interior of British Columbia. The introduction of mechanized transport put an end to their business in the 1920s, but they will always be regarded as a colourful part of the history of Ashcroft and the Cariboo.

HARPER'S MILL

Even before the railway reached Ashcroft in 1884, the first business in the area had been established. Harper's Mill began operation at the junction of the Bonaparte and Thompson Rivers in 1879. As was often done at that time, the building and machinery had been moved from a former location and set up where the owner felt he would be a better chance of success.

J.H. Scott had originally built the mill in 1865 at Parsonville, a small community just across the Fraser River from Lillooet. In that year, Scott had two thousand-pound millstones, known as French Burrs, brought around Cape Horn to San Francisco, shipped to Victoria, and brought by smaller boat up the Fraser River through Harrison Lake to Lillooet. He imported the rest of the machinery from Oregon. Scott had been growing tobacco to sell to the miners who passed through Lillooet on their way to the Cariboo gold fields, but could not make a living at this, so he set up the mill to increase his income. Unfortunately for Scott, John Marshall decided at about the same time to build a mill at the mouth of Cayuse Creek, just across the Fraser River from Parsonville. Since there was not enough business in the area for two mills, Scott soon decided to move the entire operation to Clinton. In 1866 he set up the mill at Falls, near the Pollard Ranch. This mill produced good quality flour which was shipped to the Cariboo, but not enough wheat was grown in the Clinton area to make it a viable operation, so the mill closed.

Jerome Harper, a Virginian, had come to British Columbia in the early 1860s. Being an astute businessman, Harper made a good deal of money dealing in cattle, horses, and ranching property. At one time he owned the Gang Ranch and his personal worth was estimated to be over $200,000. He bought Scott's mill, and in 1875 hired R.T. Ward, a Californian and a miller by trade, to reactivate the mill, but the same problem—scarcity of local wheat—caused Ward to look for a better location. In 1878, he decided on a site at the junction of the Bonaparte and Thompson Rivers because the CPR was surveying in this area, and there seemed to be a more reliable supply of wheat nearby.

In 1878 the Clinton mill was dismantled, the heavy timbers carefully marked so the mill could be reassembled exactly as it had been, and the entire operation, machinery and all, loaded on freight wagons and pulled by oxen down the Cariboo Road then through the Perry Ranch and Back Valley Road to the mouth of the Bonaparte. The mill was rebuilt under the supervision of Ward and James Black, construction foreman, but from the very beginning the project was dogged by misfortune.

On 14 October 1880, the "Big Slide" occurred at Black Canyon, five miles south of the mill location. An immense section of the riverbank broke away and completely blocked the Thompson River for almost two days. The water rose more than sixty feet—there was a foot and a half of water on what is now the town of Ashcroft—and posed a real threat to the mill. Ward and a crew of his workmen went to the site of the slide, and by dint of very hard work, dug a ditch which allowed water through. The natural force of the water enlarged the ditch, cutting its way through the loose gravel and alkali soil, and soon the river was running normally. But the mill building had been half submerged for over twenty-four hours, and it took considerable time and work to clean and dry it out. The owner put a sign on the mill "Big Slide, 1880, High Water Mark" which stayed in place for many years and is now on display in the Ashcroft Museum.

The mill was producing as much as fifty barrels of flour per day and because of its good quality, it sold well, but another problem arose. Although they had surveyed on both sides of the Thompson River, the CPR decided to construct its railway on the south side of the river—the mill was on the north side. Never one to be discouraged by little problems, Harper planned to build a cable ferry to take his produce across the river, but the very swift current and the poor approaches on both sides of the river made this impractical. So he decided to ship his flour to Kamloops by steamboat, but this idea died in its infancy. The *Peerless*, the only steamboat on Kamloops Lake, was owned by a company that operated a flourmill in Kamloops, and although the boat made a few trips to Ashcroft with hay and oats to be shipped northward by freighters, it carried none of the Harper Mill flour.

Despite these difficulties, the mill paid its way for several years until the demand for oats, barley and hay for the horses and mules used by the BX and freighters made these crops more valuable for local farmers, causing them to cut their wheat production drastically. The final blow to the mill occurred when roller flour from the prairies was shipped to the area. It was impossible to compete with this flour, which was of better quality and sold at a lower price than the local product.

Thaddeus Harper, who had inherited Jerome's Canadian holdings on the latter's death, imported two dozen grapevines from California. He planted these along with a number of apple trees. About a ton of grapes each season, and a good crop of apples were produced after a ram pump was installed to bring water from the Bonaparte for irrigation. Long after the property had been abandoned, these trees and vines were still bearing fruit.

Thaddeus also ran a store which stocked a good supply of dry goods and clothing, and established an excellent private library. However, he was not the businessman that his brother had been, and on his death in 1889, had much less than he had inherited. A notice of sale advertised:

> *Flour mill and machinery, store, dwelling house and out buildings...The mill is in good running order and has ample water power and valuable water priviledges (sic). The Store and Mill contain a stock of goods, agricultural implements, wagons, buggy harness, etc. Terms cash.*

The Western Canadian Ranching Company purchased the Harper holdings, and Tom Pocock of Upper Hat Creek ran the declining mill for a short time. The mill building served many purposes over the years, and was once used as an apiary. B.W. Leeson and his father were the last to try to make a go of the mill, which finally closed in 1890. Some years later, the mill was dismantled by CNR construction crews as a safety measure, and in 1944 the old millstones were salvaged by R.D. Cumming and brought to Ashcroft, where they are on display beside the old freight wagon near the bridge.

Harper's Mill (BCARS C-03486)

THE FOUNDERS OF THE VILLAGE OF ASHCROFT

The Village of Ashcroft owes its existence on its present site to the foresight of four men, hardy pioneers who saw an opportunity and grabbed it with both hands—John Christopher Barnes, F. William Brink, Oliver Hixon Evans, and William H. Bose.

Barnes, who was born in Kentucky in 1829 and moved to California in 1849, was one of the earliest of the California prospectors who flocked to the Fraser River in 1858. He tried his hand, with some success, as a prospector, cowboy and gambler. In 1859 he met William Brink from Boone County, Indiana who had just arrived in British Columbia. The two men soon became friends and partners, running a pack train to the gold fields. During this time, they also helped build trails to some of the outlying areas of the Cariboo, and were hired to survey for the CPR.

On one pack train trip, the entire party was trapped by a sudden snowstorm near Barkerville. It was impossible to get the animals out of there, so the poor creatures had to be abandoned and probably starved to death. The men had to slog their way sixty miles through three feet of snow to winter camp at Barkerville. At this point they decided to seek a new means of earning a living. They found an area that looked like promising ranching country along the Thompson River. In 1863, they pre-empted land extending from the second slough three miles east of what is now Ashcroft, along the river up to and including the present townsite, and a farm three miles south on the Highland Valley Road. Here they established a ranch, purchased horses and a large herd of cattle, and raised hay, vegetables and fruit.

Barnes and Brink married sisters, Mary Anne and Lucy Wask, two Spatsum Indian girls, and settled down to raise their families. Barnes and Mary Anne had four children: Mary Anne, James, Catherine, and John. Brink and Lucy had three children: Ellen, Billy Jr. and Margaret Emma. Billy Jr. lost a leg in a skating accident when he was quite young and always had to use a crutch. This didn't seem to handicap him, however, as he became a very good horseman and for years was a well respected hunting and fishing guide in the Highland Valley where he lived. He and his palomino were familiar figures in Ashcroft where he regularly purchased supplies. Both of his cabins were preserved as historic sites by Highland Valley Copper and can be seen today near the company office.

The third of the quartet of founders, Oliver Hixon Evans was born in Bonne County, Ohio in 1850. When he was eighteen, he and his brothers decided to drive a large herd of sheep west. It took them three long years (until 1871) to make it to British Columbia, by which time the number of sheep had increased to well over five thousand. At Savona they took the sheep, three at a time in a dugout canoe, across the Thompson River, eighteen to twenty trips a day for almost three months. The long trek finally ended when they arrived in Cache Creek and sold the animals to local farmers for a good price. With his share of the profits, Oliver bought an ox team, and in 1872 began to haul freight from Yale to Barkerville.

The last of the group, William Henry Conrad Bose was born in Hanover, Germany in 1855. He was taken to the United States by his aunt when he was only three months old. They settled in St. Louis, Missouri where Bose remained until he was sixteen when he and another young fellow ran away from home and secured jobs as freighters and muleskinners at Leadville, Colorado. After a couple of years, Bose heard the call of north and headed for British Columbia, arriving in Yale in 1875. His first job in Yale was with a merchant, Uriah Nelson, but Barnes and Brink soon hired him as swamper on their forty-five-mule pack train, a job much more to his liking. However, he only made part of one trip at this job before he and Oliver Evans had the opportunity to buy an outfit consisting of one six-yoke and two eight-yoke ox teams and wagons for $4,000. They were not required to put down any money or sign any documents. A verbal agreement was all that was necessary. Business was so good that they paid off the entire debt the next summer.

In an interview with the *Vancouver Province* in 1933, Bill Bose explained his nickname Hog Hollow Bill: "in Cariboo anyone from Missouri was just naturally called Hog Hollow, since that's a place in Missouri." He and Oliver Evans were quite a team: the stocky, stolid, bearded Evans, and the tall, broad-shouldered but gaunt Bose, with his imposing moustache, broad southern drawl, and wild sense of humour. For more than twelve years they made two trips a year between Yale and Barkerville and were, in fact, the last to haul freight out of Yale before the CPR was completed in 1886. Bose described these years in the *Province* interview:

> *I seen me start out in the spring of the year from Fort Yale when my bulls would be so thin that it would take two of them to make a good shadow and in the fall of the year, they'd all be fat as butter. It sure was a great country them days for a young fellow. We freighted stuff into the mines and got return cargo in shape of fur and hides — made money both ways. Lost an ox a trip. That set us back $125 each. They'd break a leg or get mired down while feeding. You see, we'd start out at two or three in the morning, drive until around ten-thirty, and then stop and turn the bulls out to eat — bought new bulls around Chilliwak or Fort Yale — best team I ever owned I got off old man Kipp in Chilliwak. That was Buck and Berry, best wheelers I ever owned. I mind one time making $200 pulling a boiler up at Fort Yale from a steamboat. Wa'nt nothin' there powerful enough to do the job. But I put my team, with Buck and Berry as wheelers and she sure slid up there to where we wanted her as if she had been a bale of hay. Biggest contract we ever had was*

*for contractor Onderdonk on CPR construction
— hauled a million pounds of barley from
Boston Flat to Cook's Ferry.*

Five years before the CPR was completed, Brink died and was buried on the ranch in 1879. His heirs assumed ownership of the Thompson River Ranch at the slough and Barnes retained the Mountain View (Barnes) Ranch and the land down to the river. In 1883 and 1886 Barnes acquired more crown land totalling 477 acres. Realizing the possibilities for agriculture in this arid area if enough water were available, he dammed the creek on his property, creating what is now known as Barnes Lake, and started to irrigate his fields.

But before long he found more profitable uses for his land. When he learned that the CPR tracks were to be laid right through his property, Barnes could finally hear opportunity knocking. The land, which had been on the "wrong side" of the river during the early years of the gold rush, was finally going to make a big payoff. In 1883 he and Oliver Evans used their oxen to haul 16,000 pounds of crockery, stoves, furniture, timber, kegs of nails, and cases of whiskey up the Cariboo Road. Bill Bose met them and barged the loads across the Thompson River to Barnes property, where the three men constructed the Thompson River Hotel, the first building in what was to become the town of Ashcroft.

In 1885, the CPR built a depot a considerable distance from the hotel. Never daunted by little problems, Barnes and Evans, using a windlass and mules, simply took the hotel apart and moved it across the field so it stood right opposite the station. In those early days, a room in the hotel cost one dollar per day, a meal fifty cents. The hotel was chiefly patronized by Cariboo teamsters, who appreciated the free drinks that greeted them on their arrival and got them off to a good start the next morning. Bill Bose acted as the genial hotel bartender when he was not freighting.

As the CPR tracks neared his property, Barnes, assisted by his family, Oliver, a seven-month-pregnant Ellen Evans and Billy Brink, staked out the blocks and lots of the new town of Ashcroft, once described as the best laid-out town in British Columbia. The lots then were offered for sale to the public, one being set aside for a church, but it was not until 1891 that a group of Anglicans were able to raise sufficient funds to begin the construction of St. Alban's Church.

Barnes, well known and respected "for a hundred miles around" was always willing to give a helping hand when it was needed, so there were many to mourn his passing when he died in 1900. He was buried on the ranch he had loved. His son James survived him only until 1903, and was buried beside his father. Barnes Street, Barnes Mountain, Barnes Lake, and Barnes Creek remain as memorials to the man who was instrumental in the founding of the town of Ashcroft.

Oliver and Ellen Evans lived for some time in the hotel, where their first daughter "Topsy" was born in 1884. Later, they built a log home near the hotel, then moved out to the big ranch house built by Ellen's father, William Brink, on the Butte Ranch. Their daughter Rita was born there, and in an interview many years later, fondly recalled this "family place" with its large porch, enormous silver birch trees, lilac and mulberry bushes, and little concrete fountain that Evans built for the girls. The couple had fourteen children in all, and the ranch had its own school for them and several other children in the vicinity. In the winter, they skated on the slough ice and sleighed on the hills around the river. Christmas was a particularly joyous time with the tree cut from the nearby hills decorated with candles and ornaments made by the family, a huge traditional feast, and home made gifts. Evans lived here with his wife and family until his death in 1905.

Bill Bose married Barnes' daughter Catherine in 1885 and fixed up an old granary into a comfortable home. In 1889 they took up ranching in the Highland Valley. Catherine died suddenly in 1908 at the age of forty-one years leaving eight children, including three-month old twins who died soon after their mother. Bose raised his family and ranched here for many years before he moved to Vancouver.

When he was seventy-eight years old, Bose was asked to drive an old freighter to honour Ashcroft's Golden Jubilee in the Labour Day parade. In 1933 he told the *Vancouver Province* that he was heading back to the Highland Valley to prospect up Wood Creek with Louis Antoine.

> *I been sick, but feel limber as a boy now, and the spring sunshine makes me want to get back to the bunch grass country. There was a klootchman would come out every year to Ashcroft and would have a little bag of nuggets that was purty rough and hadn't travelled fur from the feel of them. Maybe we can find some quartz up that way.*

Bose died in Lady Minto Hospital in Ashcroft on New Year's Eve, 1936 at the age of eighty-one.

"FOREVER GREAT PROSPERITY" THE CHINESE IN ASHCROFT

Between 1881 and 1884 more than ten thousand Chinese arrived in British Columbia. Most were part of the gold rush or were labourers on the CPR or road building crews. Many of them stopped over in Ashcroft for supplies and decided to remain here, some to open stores and restaurants, some to work on the local ranches. Histories of the Chinese in BC almost totally ignore their contribution to the town of Ashcroft, and yet they comprised about fifty percent of the community's population before the turn of the century. Because of the closing of the cannery in 1957 and consequent loss of a market for the tomato farmers, many moved to the west coast. By 1960, the Chinese were only about five percent of Ashcroft's population.

Wing Chong Tai ("Forever Great Prosperity") was established in Ashcroft in 1892 by two Cantonese, Chow Sing and a partner whose name seems to have been forgotten. True to its name, the business prospered and served the village well for more than ninety years. Chow Sing's brother, Chow Lung, came from China directly to Ashcroft in 1893 at the age of sixteen, and for several years worked as farm hand and house boy at Oliver Evans' Butte Ranch near Ashcroft. There he acquired knowledge of farming and ranching from Mr. Evans and learned about western cooking and baking from Mrs. Evans. Every morning, even in the hundred degree heat of summer and the forty below cold of winter, he rode bareback from town to the ranch, did his chores, and rode back to town in the evening. Subsequently, he worked on other ranches in the vicinity, and helped dig some of the first irrigation ditches in the area, some of which can still be seen.

By hard work and thrift, Chow Lung saved enough money over the next twelve years to buy a share in the Wing Chong Tai when his brother's partner decided to retire in 1905. The brothers operated the store until July 5, 1916, when it was destroyed by the fire which levelled the entire commercial district of Ashcroft.

However, Chinese carpenters were very soon at work and in short order there were more than twenty businesses back in operation, including Wing Chong Tai, Wing Wo Lung, Kwong Yueng Sing and Kwong Yee Chong. Chinatown was again alive with dances, parties, all-night teahouses, twenty-four-hour mahjong and high-stake gambling to be enjoyed by all. When the field and cannery workers arrived every harvest season, there were as many as six hundred Chinese in Ashcroft.

The social season reached its peak at Chinese New Year, a two-week celebration of feasting and drinking, culminating on January 15th when businessmen strung firecrackers the length of the street on both sides. All over town they were heard loud and clear from sundown until well past midnight and the sky glowed red with skyrockets and sparklers. Children in their Sunday best went from store to store for "Lucky Money" and returned home with a nice handful of change.

After the fire of 1916, a group of Chinese merchants got together and rebuilt the Ashcroft Hotel. The many passengers coming to town by Cariboo stage and the six daily CPR passenger trains made this a lucrative business. Often hotel patrons wanted only a place to rest for a few hours between trains and stages, so with a quick cleaning and change of linen a room could be rented three times in one day. The dining room, which boasted white linen tablecloths and quality china and silver, offered a fine menu and good service and was as popular with the local population as it was with the travellers.

Shortly after the great fire, Chow Sing retired and returned to China, turning his part of the business over to his son, Chow Ping Kew. He and Chow Lung enlarged the store to include a hand laundry, a meat department, clothing, appliances, gifts, fishing tackle, ammunition, tobacco and snuff, as well as Chinese wine and Hudson Bay rum in wooden barrels (until prohibition in the 1920s made this illegal). A toy department was added during the Christmas season. The Chows had a market garden behind the store to supply produce for their customers and also had fifty to sixty pigs, some for the meat department, but many for barbecued whole pig, Chinese style, for special family festivities.

The Chinese Drug Store was one of the most interesting and important departments of Wing Chong Tai. Because most Chinese preferred their traditional herbal to western medicine, the store stocked hundreds of herbs in small individual drawers in a very large wooden cabinet at the rear of the store. On the dispensing counter stood a small ivory balance scale, which had been brought from China specifically for weighing the herbs. Quantities were precisely prescribed by the Chinese herb doctor, who diagnosed the illness by checking the eyes, tongue and pulse of his patient. The herbs would be brewed into tea, either at home if the patient was not too ill, or at the Chinese Community Hospital for those who required more care. Cooks also took advantage of the store's large stock of herbs to add flavour to soups and meat dishes.

Many of the larger ranches in the area employed Chinese to look after their irrigation systems, essential to successful farming in this desert area. Widow Smith of Spence's Bridge hired two Chinese from Ashcroft, Lee Mong in 1905 and Toy Sing in 1932. Both men, first-class irrigators, were valued employees of the Smiths for many years. With the help of such men, Ashcroft merchants including Wing Chong Tai developed large vegetable farms during World War I. They leased land from the ranchers, brought water from mountain lakes by wooden flumes, and each year grew and shipped hundreds of rail car loads of potatoes, white beans and onions.

Chow Lung organized the potato growers so that Ashcroft potatoes were shipped under a registered name in sacks (ordered ten thousand at a time) labelled "Dry Belt Potatoes, Grown by Ashcroft Potato Growers Assoc." This assured that no inferior produce could be sold under the justly famous Ashcroft name. CPR dining cars served only carefully selected, baked Ashcroft potatoes for thirty-five cents each, a pretty hefty price considering that an entire restaurant meal could be had for under a dollar.

In 1925, a cannery was built in Ashcroft, which contracted with the local farms to supply tomatoes. Each of the four general stores in Chinatown leased two or more farms and hired Chinese from Vancouver and local Indians for the harvest. From July to mid-August, partially ripe tomatoes were shipped to Vancouver vegetable markets, and after that time the town was redolent with the aroma of vine-ripened tomatoes being canned and processed into ketchup, tomato sauce and juice. The first year the cannery ordered one million labels for their two grades of tomatoes, BX Standard and Ashcroft Choice. In early spring cold frames were constructed behind Wing Chong Tai to grow tomato bedding plants for the farms as well as for local gardeners. After World War II, Canada began importing vegetables from the United States at lower prices than the locals could sell for, so farms reverted to ranch land and many local workers left for greener pastures at the coast. In 1957 the cannery closed down. Having lost so much of their business, the Chinese merchants, one by one, moved away, leaving only Wing Chong Tai, Wing Wo Lung and a couple of restaurants.

Chow Lung's cheerful smile and much sought-after gardening hints were a special part of Ashcroft until 1960, when he died at the age of eighty-three. In 1948 Alfred Chow took over Wing Chong Tai, joined by his brother Eddie in 1952. Both of the boys were hard-working and respected members of the community. In 1981, Alfred was made the first freeman of the Village of Ashcroft, in recognition of his contributions to the town, a well-deserved honour.

Four generations of Chows operated the Wing Chong Tai for eighty-nine years, closing in June 1981, the oldest business in Ashcroft at that time. It is said that no one ever left the store hungry; there was always 'a loaf of bread, a can of beans or whatever to help them' if they were in need. It was a sad day for Ashcroft in 1985 when the old Wing Chong Tai building was demolished in the name of progress. This historic building, with its Nabob sign that was such a favourite of artists and photographers, was one of the last traces of Ashcroft's once-thriving Chinatown. In the fall of 1998, Mrs. Chow passed away, just two weeks before her hundredth birthday.

A comparable story is that of the business known as Wing Wo Lung. Chow Loy, born in Canton, China, came to this province about 1889. An uncle living in Vancouver gave him seventy-five cents and a pair of overalls, and told him to go to it. So he did. He hiked from the coast into the Cariboo, hiring out as a cook here and there along the road, notably for Judge Cornwall at Ashcroft Manor. When he arrived in Barkerville, he stayed for some time with another uncle, then returned south, stopping in Clinton where he ran a combination store, restaurant, and laundry until 1907. By this time he had accumulated enough capital to start a general store in Ashcroft in partnership with Chow Ban. They called their business Wing Wo Lung, and when Chow Ban died in 1936, Chow Loy became sole owner.

The firm was so successful and amassed such a sizable fortune in thirty-two years that it was recognized as one of the wealthiest Chinese businesses in the province. They owned farms and ranches around Ashcroft as well as wholesale produce firms in Vancouver and Victoria, and restaurants in several small B.C. towns, including Trail. Chow Loy also had large interests near Canton and made twelve trips back to China during the fifty years he lived in Canada. When he died in 1939, his body was shipped back to Canton. His widow, three sons and two daughters in Canada survived him, as did an infant daughter in China.

The arrival, in January 1910, of Dr. Sun Yat Sen, considered the father of modern China, was a high point in the history of Ashcroft Chinatown. In the week that he spent here, he found a great deal of support, both moral and financial, in his efforts to depose the corrupt Manchu Government. The tens of thousands of dollars that he raised on his Canadian visit helped him to succeed in the uprising of 1911, when he became head of the government of the new Republic of China. For many years, his political party, the Chinese Nationalist League, had an active branch in Ashcroft.

Often scorned and discriminated against, and brought up in a close-knit family society, the Chinese tended to stay close to people of their own clan or village when in foreign countries. Because of this and the fact that their frugal habits allowed them to live more cheaply and work for lower wages than whites, other workers often resented them. Labour unions pressured politicians to impose a head tax on all Chinese entering Canada, starting at $50 in 1885, and rising to $500 by 1903. Chinese were barred from public work projects and when the Chinese Immigration Act was made law in 1923, only Chinese diplomatic personnel were permitted to enter Canada. Even wives and children were not allowed to join their husbands and fathers here. The right to vote in British Columbia provincial elections, taken from the Chinese in 1874, was not restored until 1947, when the government finally extended the franchise to include Chinese and others of Asian descent.

British Columbia did not allow those of Chinese origin to enlist in the armed services during World War One, so many Chinese went to Alberta and other provinces to join up. One such was Wee Tan Louie who was born at Shuswap in 1897. He walked to the Douglas Lake Ranch when he was fourteen, where he was employed as a cowhand until 1914 when he went to Calgary to enlist in Canadian Infantry Battalion, with which he served in Italy, Belgium and Germany. Wounded in Germany, he was honourably discharged and returned to the Kamloops area, purchased an Overland car and ran a taxi service. In 1935 he and his family moved to Ashcroft and operated a trucking service through the Fraser Canyon. He also ran hay-baling business and trucked tomatoes from local farms to the cannery, and later worked on highway construction. As a returned veteran Louie, had the honour of being the first Chinese person to vote in the 1947 provincial election in BC, and he never failed to cast a ballot in every election after that.

The Chinese were often successful ranchers. Ah Duck, also known as Tong Sing, Joe Duck or Old Duck, opened a general store called Tong Sing in Cache Creek in the 1880s. He was sufficiently successful that in the early 1900s he was able to buy hundreds of acres of land in the Upper Hat Creek valley. He brought a number of men from China to help in the venture, and soon had one of the largest cattle herds in the area—over 2,000 head—as well as fields of timothy and clover for feed and a huge potato garden. In 1895, he shipped six rail car loads of Ashcroft potatoes to Vancouver.

Lee Yee was born in Victoria in 1861. Familiar only with city life, she left friends and family at the age of fourteen, to be the wife of Kwan Yip, a man more than twenty years her senior. Such an arranged marriage of a very young Chinese girl to a much older man was typical at the time, female children being considered burdens to be married off as quickly as possible. Moving to Cache Creek, a sparsely settled area with few of her own race nearby, must have been very difficult for Kwan Yee (her married name), but her good humour and friendly personality endeared her to her white neighbours whom she found to be friendly and helpful. She worked hard, helping in the operation of their general store in Cache Creek, raising a large garden, and caring for her seven children.

When her husband died in 1901, Kwan Yee was able to borrow enough money from the ranching community to put her business on a sound financial basis. She continued to run the store and grow vegetables, which she exchanged for canned goods to stock the shelves. She made sure that all her children attended school long enough to be able to read, write, and do simple arithmetic. Kwan Yee was able to repay the loans and save enough money to sell the store, take out naturalization papers, and homestead on a quarter section in the Upper Hat Creek area, about five miles from the Duck Ranch. About 1908, Kwan Yee and her children went to live with Ah Duck, and while they were together she bore him two children. She and four of her sons, all good cowboys, ran the ranch whenever Ah Duck was away on business. Kwan Yee died of tuberculosis in 1913, one of the handful of notable women who helped develop this area.

Her son, Ernie Yet, who was ranch foreman on the Duck Ranch for some time, took pride in his ability as a working cowboy. He stayed on the ranch until 1915 when he went to Vancouver. However, he found his race to be a much greater barrier to success there than it had been in the interior, and he had difficulty finding employment. He applied to join the police force, and despite the fact that he was in top physical condition and a crack shot, he had no chance of being hired. Because he spoke perfect English and three Chinese dialects, he was finally able to find employment as an interpreter for several lawyers, and as an unofficial policeman for the Freemasons.

Over the years, he ran a small trucking business, opened one of the first gas stations in Chinatown, did contract logging on Vancouver Island, acted as spokesman to the Wartime Prices and Trade Board for Chinese truckers and market gardeners, and finally worked as a taxi dispatcher. As he grew older, he often thought back to what was probably the happiest time of this life, on the ranch back in the southern Cariboo. He would get out the bullwhip he had braided many years before and crack it as he did in the old days, startling family and neighbours who thought it was a gunshot. Sadly, when he was in his seventies, still an active and vigorous man, he was beaten and robbed just behind his garage in Vancouver. He died a few hours later of a fractured skull and brain injuries.

There was much ceremony involved with a death in the Chinese community. The town was red with small pieces of paper with holes through them, the idea being that the devil had to pass through all these small holes before he could reach the deceased, and would hopefully never get to him. The *Ashcroft Journal* described one Chinese funeral procession in 1912:

> *The funeral of a chinaman was watched with much interest by the townspeople on Thursday afternoon. A table set with all the delicacies of the season, including chicken and wine, were (sic) set out on the street before the funeral cortege started, after which it was taken to the grave and deposited on the mound for the evident purpose of feeding the soul of the dead man, should he feel disposed to again eat of the things earthly. The coffin was accompanied to the cemetery by an express wagon loaded down with orientals beating symbols (sic) and drums to frighten away the evil spirits who may happen to be floating around ready to butt into the celebration uninvited.*

The fact that it did not seem important to mention the names of the "chinaman" or his family and the ironic tone of the piece are both indicative of the attitude towards Orientals at that time.

The Ashcroft Chinese Cemetery, is a sadly neglected area adjacent to the CPR tracks, its headstones almost entirely hidden by sagebrush and wild grass. Until 1942, it was the last resting-place of local Chinese who did not choose, or could not afford, to have their bodies sent back to China for burial. While some of the *Ashcroft Journal's* obituaries of local Chinese residents are woefully brief, suggesting lives that were sad and lonely, others indicate relatively successful and happy lives. They help us now to have a clearer idea of the experience of people who moved to such a totally different country than the one they were used to.

Chow Kwong Jao "was 69 years of age, married in China, and had been employed on the potato and tomato farms in this district during all his stay in the province, except for the past few years when he did very little." (Ashcroft Journal, 1942)

"Joe Gat, an aged Chinaman who might be classed as a pioneer of Ashcroft, having arrived about 25 years ago, was a clerk in the Kwong Yee Chung store in Chinatown, where he had been engaged for some time." (Ashcroft Journal, 1932)

Yip Jou Kai, a cook whose "body was discovered when he failed to show up to make breakfast. He was fifty years of age, single, but not much is known of him. On examination it was found he had a defective lung which was about half normal size. He had never complained about his health, but no doubt the lung infection was the cause of death." (Ashcroft Journal, 1941)

On Wong "is believed to have come to this country in the 1860's, and probably mined along the rivers of the Cariboo for several years. He arrived in Ashcroft in the early 1900's, and did odd jobs for the local residents, who felt he was in need of money for food. A very reliable man, at eighty he could swing an ax eight hours a day as well as a man in his thirties. In January of 1937, his hut burned to the ground, probably catching fire around the chimney, while he was cooking dinner. On Wong doggedly set about clearing away the debris, and built a dug-out shack from the materials left from the fire, in which he lived for eleven months, until a similar fire resulted in his death at the age of eighty-five. In the clothing he was wearing was found $1210.70 in cash, some of *it being old Bank of British North America bank notes that he must have been carrying around for more than twenty-five years. He was survived by a cousin in Ashcroft and a married son in China."* (Ashcroft Journal, 1936)

Long Joe had "an impressive funeral attended by a number of friends and relatives. He was about fifty years of age and came to B.C. about thirty years ago. During all that time he was engaged in potato raising in various parts of the district. He was a good citizen among the Chinese as well as the whites, and his demise has created much sympathy among all who knew him. He is survived by a wife and son in Ashcroft." (Ashcroft Journal, 1941)

Lum King "more generally known as Lum York, was a resident of Ashcroft for over thirty years, and was the well known proprietor of the York Restaurant. He was sixty-nine years of age and came to Ashcroft early in the century after being in Vancouver for some time. He married in Ashcroft and all his children attended the Ashcroft School." (Ashcroft Journal, 1939)

"Ah Hing came to British Columbia on a sailing vessel more than fifty years ago. The late Ah Hing was well known in Ashcroft, having resided here for over thirty years and a Chinaman who was highly respected in the community. The large family surviving him were born and raised in Ashcroft. Ah Hing reached British Columbia in time to work on the CPR construction. He later farmed at Ashcroft and for a number of years was foreman at the old Lehman ranch, better known as the Thompson place. He retired in 1923."
(Ashcroft Journal, 1939)

These and other Chinese residents of Ashcroft, each in their own way, contributed to the prosperity and development of the community and played an important part in moulding the distinctive character of Ashcroft.

Crossing the bridge at Ashcroft (BCARS C-01274)

THE GREAT FIRE

July 5th, 1916 was a typical summer day in Ashcroft, with the blue sky clear and bright, the blazing sun, and the temperature more than 110 degrees (43 Celsius). The Wednesday business of the bustling little community carried on as usual. The red and yellow BX fresh-air taxis brought passengers from the Cariboo; the CPR trains brought freight and passengers from the coast and from the east; Wing Chong Tai and Harvey Bailey served their many regular customers; cattle were herded into town for shipment to the packers; neighbours chatted over the back fence, and businessmen in the cafes discussed the war. At closing time the locals went home to dinner, the strangers to the bar or the cafe.

At seven o'clock the calm was shattered by the frenzied tolling of the fire bell. Men, women and children dashed from their homes, visiting businessmen from their hotels. Passengers on the CPR train arriving from Vancouver were greeted by the sight of smoke and flames belching from the second floor of the Ashcroft Hotel. The volunteer fire department rushed equipment to the site, hose and nozzle at the ready, but before they could throw enough water at the fire, the roof was ablaze. They were forced to retreat from their positions as flames moved toward them and the searing heat made further efforts impossible. The hotel was by now an inferno and was abandoned to its fate.

But worse was to come. The hot west wind spread the fire to the tinder-dry cedar roofs so rapidly that the firemen could not possibly move their equipment quickly enough to be of any use. Just next door to the hotel, the Morgan & Murphy law offices and the Bank of British North America were soon in flames. The Harvey Bailey store was the next victim. Although the exterior was brick, inside were wooden floors, partitions and furniture as well as fifty thousand dollars worth of merchandise that was quickly devoured by the flames. The Grand Central Hotel was next, and paint began to blister and windows crack on buildings on both sides of Railway

Avenue. The frame structures caught fire like so much tinder and their burning cedar shingles, blown by the strong wind, spread the fire very rapidly. The reflection of the conflagration could be seen as far away as Walhachin and Savona.

Years later in a taped interview, Ashcroft residents Mabel and Cliff Walker recalled that the women of Ashcroft formed a bucket brigade from the CPR pump beside the tracks to fight the fire, while many of the men were busy hauling liquor out of the hotel. Most of the business district was destroyed, but the west wind kept the flames and sparks away from the residential section of town, and few homes were lost. However, the business district and Chinatown had been almost totally wiped out by the time the fire burned itself out as it reached the river.

An unconfirmed story suggests that a guest of the Ashcroft Hotel started the tragic series of events when he fell asleep while smoking and his mattress caught fire. Some others suggested arson. Whatever the cause, the toll of the fire was enormous. In addition to the two hotels and the Harvey Bailey block, buildings destroyed included the Fire Hall, three barns, the Robert Stoddart shop and lumber yard, the Huston livery, the J. Warden barber shop, the F. Kaltenbeck jewellery store, the law offices of James Murphy and R. Morgan, the Bank of British North America, the post office, the telegraph office, Engeman's pool room, Koelkenbeck's moving picture theatre, M. Dumond hardware, Campbell ice cream parlour and stationery, Charles Gibson meat market, Cargile Hotel, Smith and Bryson blacksmith shop, Northern Crown Bank, Inland Express Company office and barn, George Stuart harness emporium, Wing Chong Tai, Wing Wo Lung, Lin Kee and Hop Wo stores as well as many other Chinatown businesses. Residences lost were those of H. Koelkenbeck, W.O. Huston, D.T.H Sutherland and Mrs. J. Newland.

Some furniture and personal possessions were rescued from the homes, but there was no time to remove the merchandise and equipment from the businesses before the fire got to them. In the short time that it took the blaze to destroy the business section, over $250,000 in damages was incurred—a very considerable sum in 1916—only $70,000 of which was covered by insurance. Those who lost the most were Harvey Bailey, Steve Tingley, M. Dumond, Smith & Bryson, and the Ashcroft and Grand Central Hotels.

Citizens patrolled the whole night of July 5th and the early morning hours of July 6th to make sure that the smouldering embers did not come back to life and devour the residential section of Ashcroft as well. The total desolation that met the eye of the population of Ashcroft in the morning was enough to discourage even the most optimistic. Merchants and tradesmen could be seen searching through the rubble of their once thriving businesses for any articles of value that might have been left undamaged, but to little avail. By some quirk of fate, a few buildings in the centre of town were left standing: the *Ashcroft Journal* office, the Harvey Bailey warehouse, the B.C. Express office and stables, the Rosenburg store and warehouse, the CPR waiting room, and a few small buildings.

On 8 July, the *Ashcroft Journal* reported that a dozen entrepreneurs had already re-established their firms in these buildings, and an advertisement assured customers that the Harvey Bailey store was open for business as usual in its warehouse. The Bank of British North America, the Inland Express Company, the James Murphy law office, the Northern Crown Bank, the post office, the commercial telegraph office, R. Morgan, the jeweller, the barber, and M. Dumond reopened almost immediately in the few remaining buildings, albeit in cramped quarters.

Of course, these were but temporary arrangements. Soon most of the heaps of bricks, twisted metal and piles of ashes had been cleared away, the gaping holes in the ground filled in, and construction started on new buildings. The insurance companies paid off promptly, and the businessmen of Ashcroft did the rest. By mid August carpenters and other tradesmen were busily rebuilding the business section of Ashcroft except for the Ashcroft and Grand Central Hotels. Although none of the Chinese establishments were covered by insurance, here too reconstruction was soon in full swing and, in short order, Chinatown was back in business.

An article in the *Ashcroft Journal* in early November 1916 complained that there had been no effort made to reconstruct the Ashcroft and Grand Central hotels, and that consequently Ashcroft was losing hundreds of dollars every day because of lack of accommodation for travellers. Finally, in 1917 a group of Chinese merchants rebuilt the Ashcroft Hotel, which for many years did a thriving business catering to the many travellers who arrived on the trains and stages every day.

There have been other fires in Ashcroft, but none of the magnitude of the 1916 conflagration. Sadly, fire is a recurring theme in the history of many communities in British Columbia. Many cities and town have been virtually destroyed: Barkerville and Victoria in 1868, Vancouver in 1886, New Westminster in 1898, and Fernie in 1908 to name just a few. As in Ashcroft, the extensive destruction was usually attributable to the wood construction of most of the buildings, inadequate fire-fighting equipment and lack of water. As in Ashcroft, the local people were soon at work as new and better communities rose from the ashes.

OUTDOOR SPORTS

Outdoor sports were an important part of life in the interior of British Columbia from the early days. Enthusiastic followers of the "sport of kings," Clement and Henry Cornwall built a race track at Ashcroft Manor in 1865 and imported thoroughbred mares and studs for breeding saddle and race horses. They held spring and fall race meets, including the Ashcroft Derby, the Lytton Steeple Chase, and the Yale Steeple Chase at which Judge Matthew Begbie acted as steward. The Cornwalls and other local residents were joined by racing enthusiasts from all over the colony for these major social events, which incidentally brought good business to their roadhouse. The racing fans would spend as much as $1,500 during the two days that the meets usually lasted.

Even more important to the Cornwalls were their so-called "fox" hunts, which they held for twenty years starting in November 1868 when they imported two pair of foxhounds from England. Most of their spare time during the winter months was spent in the chase, using coyotes in place of foxes. In addition to being more readily available than foxes, the coyotes made for better sport because of their speed. Horsemen from all over British Columbia joined the Cornwalls and their visiting English gentry in these hunts. Clement Cornwall's enthusiasm for the hunt and its social significance is clear in the following excerpt from his journal:

> *[H]owever attractive other pursuits and sports may be in their way, hunting must be placed first and the rest NoWhere!...in B.C., a country utterly devoid of the rational recreation and amusement indulged in elsewhere by the upper classes of society...it is easy to conceive what the hounds were to us in the winter. They were the object of life — they were life itself!*

John Christopher Barnes, one of the original founders of the town of Ashcroft, true to his Kentucky ancestry was also a lover of horses and horse racing. In 1886 he organized horse races through the middle of the new town of Ashcroft, down the main street and around what buildings there were at the time, or from the centre of town to the cemetery. There was a variety of races: saddle horse, stock horse, half mile, quarter mile, Klootchman, Indian, ladies, children's, pony and relay races, turning stakes, and the Ashcroft Derby which was "open to the world", with prize money of $100 for first, $50 for second. These proved to be very popular, and continued for many years in conjunction with the annual fair and Spud City Potlach Days. These popular two-day events attracted people from many miles around and sleeping accommodations were at a premium. The three hotels were filled and the surrounding area was covered with tents. In the early days there was some bronc riding, but this was pretty dangerous at the time, there being no corrals or fences to contain the bucking horses which would often charge into the spectators on the board walks. Later proper facilities were constructed, calf roping, steer riding, and barrel racing were added to the festivities and the Ashcroft Stampede was born, still one of the highlights of the year in the village.

Baseball, lacrosse, and football have also been important activities in Ashcroft since before the turn of the century, in competition with Kamloops, Clinton, Merritt and Savona. There was keen rivalry between the towns, but when the game was over, there was time for supper and a dance for the visiting team which usually stayed for the night, travelling being difficult and time consuming.

Winter sports were an important part of the Ashcroft scene from very early times. A frozen slough two miles east of town next to the Thompson River was used for both curling and skating in the late 1880s, and a well used rink it was. The February 1892 *Inland Sentinel* reports that "a splendid rink has been made by flooding from the (CPR) water tank a large space on the main street of Ashcroft between Cargile House and the railway track, and great sport for skaters young and old is on every day and night." This practice was followed for many years and the ice was used for curling when the slough was not usable. The main disadvantage to this clever scheme was that cinders from the many steam locomotives that passed through town would pockmark the ice, which did not interfere too much with the skating but made it very difficult for the skip to choose the correct ice. Who could tell where the stone would finally come to a stop?

At the same time hockey became an important part of the winter scene, and continues to have wide support in the community. Skating carnivals and competitions are also recorded from the turn of the century.

The early devotees of the sport of curling had neither the carefully matched rocks nor the scientifically designed brushes that seem to be essential for today's game. Wooden blocks of roughly the same size and shape were taken to the local tinsmith to be covered with galvanized iron. After iron handles were attached, the curler was ready to go. It was several years before Ashcroft curlers felt it necessary to replace these with "stanes" which they ordered directly from Scotland. An ordinary kitchen corn broom was used for sweeping, more to clean snow and frost off the rough outdoor ice surface than to further the progress of the rock.

The July 29, 1899 issue of the B.C. Mining Journal announced the formation of a curling club in the town. It is believed that only Golden had an organized curling club before this time. That same year, plans were made for the construction of a curling and skating rink on Bancroft Street, next to the fair grounds, part of which could be used as a bath house in the summer months.

Interest in curling increased over the years. In 1904 the Ashcroft Journal said: "At almost any hour of the day or night that enough players can be brought together, a game is on." In 1906 the newspaper claimed that Ashcroft "had more lovers of curling than any town its size in B.C." The club usually showed a small financial surplus ($93.10 in 1907; $78.00 in 1908). In 1911, a skating and curling facility complete with lighting was built. This was used for forty-five years until 1955 when it was replaced by a new curling rink and a separate skating arena. Natural ice was used during the first year of operation, but artificial ice was installed in 1956 thanks to volunteer labour and financing. It is noteworthy that the upkeep of the curling rink, including ice making, is still taken care of entirely by volunteers from the local community.

Courtesy Ashcroft Museum   *Curlers at Ashcroft, circa 1900*

ENTERTAINMENT IN EARLY ASHCROFT

In the April 27, 1935 edition of the *Ashcroft Journal*, we read:

> *In the 1890s no movies, no gramophones, no radios. One wonders what the Ashcroft aborigines did with their time; but, across the gap that spans the years, we read of frequent visits from travelling troup shows of all kinds, good, bad, and indifferent. Among those who came here periodically one remembers the Harry Lindley show, a 'Barn-Stormer' who got to be like one of the family after a while. Then there was the circus with its side shows and 'skin games' to clean up the easy marks. And a story is told of one citizen who spent $40 at two-bits a throw in efforts to buy a cake of soap with a five dollar bill wrapped around it. But 'them were the days.'*

The "Ashcroft aborigines" were very good at making their own entertainment. Many people sang or were able to play an instrument, and musical evenings were a common and enjoyable part of life in private homes and in town and church halls. In almost every edition of the *Journal*, there is an item about the socials and bazaars and the good food and music they featured.

Before the turn of the century there was an obvious need for a community hall for dances, concerts and other entertainments. In the 1890s, the Town Hall, known locally as the Opera House, was built on land donated by J.C. Barnes. It was a well used building, playing host to such varied activities as dances, an evening with E. Pauline Johnson, a company of twenty-two from the Metropolitan Opera Company, school Christmas concerts, and many musical evenings by local musicians. It was later used as a movie theatre, and the building still stands today.

One of the social highlights of the year was the January banquet of the Yale-Lillooet Pioneer Society, which was formed in Ashcroft on January 13, 1889. Forty to fifty men who had come to British Columbia between 1858 and 1864 met in Ashcroft to enjoy a truly magnificent banquet and no doubt to talk about the good old days. A list of their names reads like a "Who's Who" of interior B.C. history.

The Ashcroft Fall Fair was started in October 1887 and attracted many visitors to the town to enjoy the fine display of livestock, vegetables, fruit, flowers, needlework, and fine arts. There was even contest for the prettiest baby. Bands from Kamloops and Fountain entertained during the day, there were sports competitions and a dance was held in the evening. A large exhibition building stood for many years near the Thompson River, and the fair was a popular part of Ashcroft life for fifteen years. Since then it has had a checkered history, as it was changed from poultry show to flower and horticultural show, to Potlatch Days and back again to Fall Fair.

Dances were a very popular form of entertainment in the towns of the B.C. interior. Typical was the Ashcroft IOOF Annual Ball of January 1895. It began with the Town Hall being carefully decorated with evergreens, flags, Chinese lanterns, and emblems of the lodge. Hotels and private homes were filled with guests from far and wide who began to arrive the morning of January 24.

Dressed in their best, everyone was in the hall when the band struck up the grand march at 8:30 p.m., and dancing continued until midnight supper, catered to by Mrs. Glencross at the Cariboo Exchange Restaurant and Mr. Lyne at the Ashcroft Hotel. The Hautier Band began to play again about 1 a.m. and it was not until 5 a.m. on January 25 that everyone went off to enjoy a few hours sleep before the festivities resumed. At 2 p.m. the windows of the Town Hall were covered, footlights and chandeliers were lit for the afternoon entertainment of songs, instrumental music, recitations and readings and a play, a farce called "A Quiet Family". By 8:30, the band was playing for another night of dancing, which continued until 4 a.m. on January 26 when the merrymaking finally concluded. The town of Clinton still carries on this tradition with its annual stampede ball in May.

These people had great stamina and obviously enjoyed their social life. This is illustrated in a story about an Ashcroft man, Tom Kirkpatrick, who played for a dance at Cook's Ferry (now Spence's Bridge), where he lived at the time. At 9 p.m. Tom tuned his fiddle, applied resin to his bow, and was ready for action. A man named Hanse provided rhythm with a wooden tub and a pair of tablespoons. A great time was had until about 11 p.m. when the E string on the violin broke. With no spare and unable to find anything that would work as a makeshift string, Kirkpatrick continued to play, and play well, with only three strings until four o'clock the next morning when another string snapped. With a shot of brandy to encourage him, he made acceptable music with two strings, although the hairs in his bow were fast thinning out. For the final square dance, Kirkpatrick put resin directly onto the wood of the bow, but he finally quit when his D string gave out. It was time for flapjacks and a little sleep.

CHURCHES

In the early days of the Cariboo-Chilcoten, the religious needs of the people were met by itinerant missionaries, who came on foot or on horseback over difficult trails from Kamloops, Vancouver and the Nicola Valley. These dedicated men represented many religious denominations, but all were concerned with the spiritual well-being of both the native and settler communities they served. Religion, with or without church buildings, played a central role in the family and social life of this sparsely settled area.

Reverend H. Irwin, an Anglican priest, was one of the first to visit the Ashcroft Manor in 1860. There being no churches in the area, he and other missionaries stopped at ranches, homesteads, trading posts and such roadhouses and hotels as there were. They conducted their services in settlers' homes or in the dining rooms or saloons of the inns. Innkeepers would cut off the drinks and insist, often in rather non-church like terms, that the customers take part in the service. These were often a little unconventional when the bar patrons got too much into the spirit of the occasion. One story has it that one very inebriated fellow sang "Nearer My God to Thee" very boisterously throughout an entire service.

When the CPR was built, many of these men of God were given passes and went from station to station, sometimes travelling and preaching in box cars. The conditions under which they lived and worked were pretty primitive much of the time, but they carried on spreading the gospel and ministering to the natives, miners, businessmen, settlers and adventurers who populated the B.C. interior. The services brought different benefits to each individual—a deepening of faith, memories of the homes they had left, a sense of peace in a rugged land, or simply a welcome, if brief, relief from a life of hardship and heavy work.

Before the turn of the century, the Chinese (who made up about half of the population Ashcroft) continued to follow their Buddhist faith individually or in small groups in their homes. Although they did not build a temple, they established their own cemetery for those who did not choose to have their remains shipped back to China. This helped them to preserve their culture in this new land.

St. John of Latin Gate was the first church in the Ashcroft area, and was built by the Cornwall brothers at Ashcroft Manor. This Anglican Church, of log construction, was not only for the use of the Cornwalls, but for the religious education of the workers and their families on their ranch. By 1900 it was sadly in need of repairs, and was moved to the Cornwall Indian Reserve. Since then, the members of the Indian Band have done considerable work in restoring this charming old church.

The "Review of Life in the Town of Ashcroft" in the *Inland Sentinel* of December 1889 observes that in "the matter of religious services, the town of Ashcroft does not fare as well as many other towns in the interior. But it is anticipated a change will soon be made." Indeed, the next two years saw two additional churches constructed.

The Anglican congregation in the town of Ashcroft, directed by the Diocese of New Westminster under Bishop Sillatoe, was a missionary parish without a church or resident minister. Services were held in the Ashcroft Hotel. As the population increased, with many of the businessmen and ranchers coming from England, the need for an established Anglican Church became more pressing. A lot had been set aside for a church by J.C. Barnes when the town was surveyed in 1884, but it was not until 1891 that sufficient money was accumulated by donations and various fund-raising projects to start construction on St. Alban's Anglican Church, named after St. Alban the Martyr.

W. Higginbottom was contracted to build the church for a sum of $500. The doors and windows, designed by Higginbottom, were built in Vancouver, and the pews and altar rail were built by the contractor himself. In three months the job was completed, and the vicarage was built shortly after. The very fine interior fittings were gifts from various sources. The Litany desk and brass railings came from France. The altar frontals, brass cross and alms dish from England; the hangings, linen and vases from St. Alban's in London; the altar cloths from the Old Country Society. The silver wafer box and cruet, plaques and other items were provided by the townspeople of Ashcroft. The church bell, purchased in England for $400, was used as a fire alarm until the fire hall was built in 1899. The first stained glass window was installed nearly a century later in 1981 and a second in 1991.

By 1892, there were enough residents of other faiths to consider building a second church, this time Presbyterian. A lot on Bancroft Street was donated jointly by J.J. McKay and the CPR for the project, and the Trustees and Building Committee purchased the adjoining lot for a manse. It was decided that the total cost of the church, completely furnished, should be $1,500.

The Presbytery of Columbia was asked for approval and a loan of $600. Various social functions were held and townspeople of all beliefs contributed generously so that $1,950 was ultimately added to the fund, and construction was soon under way. Dedicated in 1893, Zion Church was used by both Presbyterian and Methodist congregations until 1897 when the Methodists were able to build their own church.

The three denominations, Anglican, Presbyterian and Methodist lived in an atmosphere of cooperation and goodwill. Typical of the times was one Anglican woman who faithfully attended St. Alban's every Sunday morning, then, just as faithfully, hurried over to the Presbyterian Church and later to the Methodist Church to play the organ for their services.

In 1925 the Methodist and United faiths amalgamated to form Zion United Church. In 1926, the Methodist Church building was moved to the rear of Zion Church and used as the Sunday school. Although the interior has been renovated, the early charm of Zion has been carefully preserved, retaining the lofty ceilings and the original kerosene lamps. After several years, many of the Chinese converted to the Christian faith, most to the United Church, starting with the children who attended Sunday school, followed after some time by the adults who joined the church.

The Oblate Missionaries, who ministered to the Bonaparte Indians built St. Louis Church, the first Roman Catholic Church in the district, on the Bonaparte Reserve in the 1880s. In Ashcroft, missionaries from the Redemptorist Mission Centre held services in the lobby of the Ashcroft Hotel using the Coke machine as an altar until 1941, when the Mason brothers, who owned the hotel, sold a lot to the Redemptorist Fathers. They also gave them a double garage which, when moved to the lot, was remodelled into a church for the eight parishioners.

Father McKenna, using the Bishop's grant of $175 and many willing volunteers of all faiths, was the impetus behind the project. The move posed a couple of problems. The need for a permit had been overlooked, but the mayor quickly provided one in mid-move, and then the building, which was on skids pulled by a cherry-picker, got stuck on the railway tracks. Since many trains go through Ashcroft every day, there was no time to lose. The unflappable Father McKenna located a forklift, the building was freed, and the move completed before the next locomotive rumbled down the tracks. When the building was finally settled on its lot, the walls were lined with plywood, a floor laid, an altar and benches installed. Sadly, Father McKenna had been sent to another parish by the time the church was ready to be consecrated.

This building served the Ashcroft parish, which had increased to twelve members, for eighteen years. After work on the Highland Valley mine was started, it was felt that the expected increase in population would make a larger church desirable. The Bishop gave a grant for the construction. Brezina Contractors were hired, and assisted by volunteers from all religious denominations, they completed St. Gerard Roman Catholic Church in 1959, when it was dedicated and blessed by the Bishop from Kamloops.

To this day the Anglican, United and Catholic churches serve the Ashcroft community and display the same cooperation and mutual respect that made their development possible.

Moving the Methodist Church (BCARS C-01227)

THE ASHCROFT JOURNAL: ONE HUNDRED YEARS OF RECORDED HISTORY

Carefully preserved in the *Ashcroft Journal* office is a fragile and yellowed piece of paper--the only copy of an important piece of our history. It is the first issue of the *British Columbia Mining Journal*, dated Thursday, 9 May 1895. Small in size, a four-page, seven-column publication costing five cents a copy or two dollars a year, the *British Columbia Mining Journal* was greeted with enthusiasm by residents of Ashcroft and district. A new name—the *Ashcroft Journal*—was adopted by the end of the century. The publication has not missed an edition in over one hundred years. Though the *Ashcroft Journal* was not the first newspaper in the province, it is now the oldest continuously operating weekly publication in British Columbia.

Dr. Frank Stewart Reynolds, and his partner A.H.S. Sroufe, explained in the first issue that they had founded the *Journal:*

> *...for the purpose of giving weekly news regarding the rich placer and quartz mining industries of British Columbia. After carefully viewing the situation the publishers decided that no other point in the province could offer the facilities for the gathering of mining news from the various districts that Ashcroft could, and while the Mining Journal will endeavor to give the Ashcroft region a good and reliable gist of weekly news, it will be principally devoted, as stated above, to gathering and publishing happenings in Cariboo, Yale, Lillooet and Kootenay mining districts, and will endeavor to fill a long-felt want in the province, i.e. to be distinctly a mining journal...*

Born in Fond du Lac, Wisconsin in 1853, Reynolds grew up and was educated in Wisconsin. He started his working life as a schoolteacher, but soon returned to university, and earned his M.D. at Rush College in 1876. He practised medicine in Hartford, Wisconsin until 1886, when he moved to Tacoma, Washington and then to Alaska. There he developed his life long interest in mining when he located the Silver Queen mine. He stayed in the north as general manager of Silver Queen Mining Company until a decline in the silver market in 1891 forced its closure. Reynolds resumed his medical career, and was appointed county physician in Loomis in Okanagan County, Washington, a position he held for two years.

Home of the Ashcroft Journal since 1898
(Courtesy Ashcroft Museum)

His enthusiasm for mining led him to the Cariboo in 1894. He and his family drove the five hundred miles by team and buckboard to Quesnelle, where they spent the summer. There he helped to establish the Quesnelle River Hydraulic Gold Mining Company, and he acquired interests in the Beaver Mouth properties and the Lightning Creek Gold Gravel & Drainage Company. After the Quesnelle River operation was sold Reynolds returned for a short time to Wisconsin, but was back in British Columbia in 1895, settling in Ashcroft. He sent to Loomis where he owned the plant of a small weekly paper, and had the entire plant, consisting of a small job press, an old-fashioned Washington press, a few cases of type, and an imposing stone, loaded on a freight wagon, brought to Ashcroft and installed in a shed adjoining a blacksmith shop.

This was the beginning of the *British Columbia Mining Journal*. In 1898 it moved to its present location, a building which survived the Great Fire of 1916, and today is one of the historic sites of Ashcroft. As circulation increased, a Prouty press, a very modern piece of equipment at the time, was installed. The "power" for this press was provided by a Chinese man named Mow, while a member of the editorial staff fed in the paper and periodically checked the ink supply. Later Mow was promoted to feeder, and a younger Oriental provided the muscle.

Containing mostly mining news, not just about the Cariboo but from other parts of Canada, the United States, and from as far away as Africa, the paper was credited with creating a new feeling of optimism about mining in the province. Considerable insight into the problems and details of mining at the time can be gained by glancing through these early editions.

> *The Finch Mining and Dredging Company which are working on the Fraser, about five miles north of Lytton, are said to be making about $20 an hour, the cost of operating the plant being some $20 a day. There are about 500 men at work on the bars between Lytton*

and Lillooet, and these average from $2.50 to $6 a day with the rocker.

Stern and uncompromising measures should at once be put in force to prevent the flagrant acts of theft known as "claim jumping" and to punish perpetrators. Several valuable claims have of late been "jumped" in the Trail Creek district, and notably the Great Western and Golden Chariot. These claims were purchased by Messrs. Burke & Jones of Spokane. Since the purchase the claims have been jumped and renamed. The rightful owners, however, have determinedly signified their intention of maintaining their right of title in the law courts. The Tribune thus notes: "Judge Walkem should preside at the next session of court in the Kootenay. Afterwards there would be few jumpers."

It is estimated that since the discovery of gold in the province Cariboo alone has added $60,000,000 in dust to the world's store of the yellow metal...When the easily accessible diggings had been overrun by the white miners the output fell off, but Chinamen and Indians and hundreds of white men — there had been formerly thousands — continued to wash the gravel along the creeks and rivers tributary to the Fraser, Thompson and Peace Rivers...The advent of the Canadian Pacific Railway made transportation of provisions to the mines much cheaper, and consequently where an ounce of gold a day would hardly pay the old-timer, $5 or $6 a day would pay the latter day miners, and mining again resumed on a large scale.

Early issues of the *Journal* relegated local news to the status of fillers, but relied mainly on Ashcroft enterprises, such as Harvey-Bailey, the Ashcroft Hotel, F.W. Foster, and Cargile

House for the advertising revenues that kept it afloat. Gradually hometown news took on more importance, and in May 1899 the publication became the *Ashcroft Journal,* dealing with regional events and issues, as well as mining news.

In the early editions, news items ran one into the other, with no obvious separation of ideas, not even paragraphs, as in this exerpt the *Journal* of 23 November 1898 :

> *ASHCROFT — Freight is still moving north by wagon, the entire distance to Barkerville. The weekly quadrille club meetings are pleasant and entertaining. John Wilson shipped several carloads of cattle to the coast. November this year so far has been like the month of May, warm and pleasant and no severe frosts, it is likely to continue to Christmas. On Tuesday 61 head of thoroughbred Shorthorn bulls arrived from Ontario for the B.C. Cattle Co. Mr. Prentice, manager of the ranch says the shipments made from the ranch recently were a complete success financially and that many more will follow this. There is quiet talk around Ashcroft of forming a Masonic Lodge. D. Murphy an old timer from 141 Mile House was in town to meet his son who has just been admitted to the bar.*

The type was set by hand during Reynold's time at the paper, his son and daughter performing this task as they got old enough. Sroufe moved to Seattle in 1896, but Reynolds ran the paper until 1902, when he sold out and moved to Vancouver, where he started the *Weekly Ledger,* then to Ladysmith and Nanaimo where he also operated local papers. The next owner, J.E. Knight, installed a monoline typesetter. In 1908 he sold to D.W. Rowlands, who in turn sold to R.D. Cumming in 1912.

In the sixty-six years they owned the *Journal,* three generations of the Cumming family saw many changes in the paper and in the town of Ashcroft. They installed a linotype, started using photographs, changed from reporting just social news to "hard" news, added headlines and generally modernized the *Journal.*

The Cumming family had been in British Columbia about ten years when the *Journal* was founded. In 1885 Robert D. Cumming, age fourteen, sailed from Glasgow with his parents William and Elizabeth Cumming, and his brother William Jr. They travelled by ship, CPR box car and Barnard's Express to Pavilion, where they lived with Elizabeth's brother, William Lee, and helped him in his grist mill for about a year. Lillooet was their next stop. There they operated a general store for twenty-four years and were agents for the BX. In his late teens, Robert went back to Scotland to attend Edinburgh University. On his return to Canada, he and his brother worked in their parents' store, and hauled freight from Lillooet and flour from Pavilion to Ashcroft. They also had a photography studio and continued to help their uncle in his mill, which they bought in the late 1890s.

Robert opened a general store in Ashcroft in 1904, sold the mill in 1906, and bought the *Journal* in 1912. Robert Cumming's business activities did not end with the purchase of the newspaper. He would also own at various times an ice cream parlour, a grocery-dry goods store, a theatre, a real estate and insurance office, and a commercial print shop. In addition, under the pseudonym "Skookum Chuck," he wrote three books and a good deal of poetry, some of which appeared in the paper. Robert and his wife Margaret had four sons and one daughter. All the boys worked in the *Journal* office after school. Robert (usually known as R.D.) bought the *Fraser Valley Record* in 1923 and, with sons Tom and Lew as co-publishers, also established the *Abbotsford-Sumas-Matsqui News* and the *Agassiz Advance* in the early 1930s.

R.D. Cumming successfully ran the *Journal* until ill health forced him to turn it over to Tom in 1936. When Tom decided to move to Vancouver in 1945, R.D. took over again for a year until Lew became the publisher in 1946. Lew continued the tradition established by R.D. of including his poetry in the newspaper, writing under the heading "Chips Off the Old Block." In 1959, a third generation of the Cumming family, Lew Jr., became editor-publisher. The Cumming family published the *Journal* until 1978, when it was purchased by the present owners, Cariboo Press. After the sale to the Cariboo Press, Lew Jr. continued to operate The Print Shoppe for several years and remained actively interested in the preservation of Ashcroft history.

During the sixty-six years they published the *Journal,* the Cumming family were successful in their goal of reporting in a "straight forward, easily understood manner." They believed it should be "the goal of any newspaper that the populace, young and old, educated and average, may read and understand." But they did more than this. Reading through some of the early editions, one gets an intimate sense of the times from the personal observations and poetry that are interspersed with the news items. That the community appreciated their efforts was evident in the support they received from subscribers and advertisers over those many years.

R.D.'s "Looking Backward" column was one of the readers' favourites. It recalled special events in the area and in his own life with warmth and charm and provides much insight into the character of the man. Number 7—"A Hunting We Will Go"—brought to life an expedition on the steep and winding trails on Pavilion Mountain, Mount Chililta and Mount Soues, with brother William and Arthur Martley of the Grange Ranch near Pavilion. He described the climb in some detail, concluding with the following:

> *We cast our weary bodies on a grassy spot surrounded by a number of stunted fir trees. Shortly there was a rustle in the trees and a young doe appeared at a short distance. In a moment the three brave and enthusiastic*

hunters were on their feet pointing rifles at the game. Shots were fired, in the course of seconds, the doe fell on the ground, and the brave hunters dashed forward to despatch the game. They paused just as hastily, however, when a young fawn darted from the timbers and began prancing around and around the mother as though expecting she would jump to her feet. Since there was no response, the fawn suddenly spied the hunters and disappeared into the woods. It was my last big game hunt.

Since being taken over by Cariboo Press, the *Journal* has had several editors: Esther Darlington, Ida Makaro, Brian Belton, Ken Alexander, and at the time of writing, Barry Tait. It is still a fine small town paper with a personal touch, covering events and issues of interest to residents of the town and nearby communities.

****

On the following pages is a small sample of poetry by R.D. and Lew Cumming, both of whom frequently included their poetry in the *Ashcroft Journal* during their time as owner-publishers.

SOMEWHERE IN FRANCE

Somewhere in France a voice I hear;
Somewhere in France a face I see;
Above the roar of guns, and clear
Through smoke and fume, they come to me.

Somewhere in France a boy I know;
My joy, my blood, my life is he,
Attuned for weal, or steeled for woe;
Down in a trench he smiles at me.

He juggles night and day with death,
Yet clings to faith in victory;
He lives with drawn, abated breath
Taut moments of uncertainty.

But hold! I see him charge the guns
Immune from shot and shell and gas,
Then gain the trenches of the Huns,
And to the German border pass.

I see him strike, I hear his call;
Look at his bright, triumphant eye;
Around him comrades fight and fall;
Look how he waves his banner high!

My God, I see him pierced! He falls!
He dies! The battle rolls away;
Then comes from the earth those groans and calls
That mock the clamor of the fray.

Then come the ambulances, led
In one long, solemn, gallant stream;
They cull the living from my dead —
I wake, behold it is a dream!

WILD ANIMALS 1915

(Suggested on seeing the B.C. Big Game pictures at the Movies)

They are the children of the earth,
The naked earth and snow;
The pathless forest gives them birth,
Out of the rocks they grow.

They know no past to blight their day,
Inspect no future view;
They rise spontaneous from the clay
And fall spontaneous too.

For land or lease they battle not,
No claims are filed or kept;
Their fortune is the food unbought,
They gather step by step.

The flower, the fruit, the cliff, the creek
They know by sight and smell;
They have no word to think and speak,
By which to know and tell.

Themselves, unnamed, unruled, unclassed,
No purpose of their own,
Unrescued from their dismal past,
Just like the tree and stone.

Hard bosomed on the rock and clay,
Cold bedded on the snow;
They live the hour, the night, the day,
And that is all they know.

ALL MAKING GOOD BUT ME

They are all "making good " but me —
    I am a stone
That the masons have thrown
Out from the flawless and free.

Fettered I see men advance —
    "Jack," the old "stager"
    Is C.E.F. Major.
"Jim" is a Captain in France.

What basis of purpose in me?
    Am I a blind mole
    Just eating a hole
Down through my life to eternity?

Afar I see men ascending —
    "Billy" Magee
    Is an M.P.P
I a utensil appending.

Am I a toad in the mud?
    In efforts to climb
    I spring from the slime
I rise but fall with a thud.

"Tom" is a Mayor elected —
    Friends once so kind,
    Have left me behind.
"Dick" was a consul selected.

I am hungry and thirsty in vain,
    I try to believe
    That I live to achieve,
That I'm not a mere link in a chain.

They are all "in the swim" but I,
    I cannot define
    How to keep up in line
No matter how much I try.

THE FLEET 1915

The fleet! the fleet! the British fleet
Which vigils firth, and shire, and mull;
Protects our merchant marine — makes
The British Empire possible!

Which moves in a mysterious way
Our would-be masters to astound;
Which conquers here today, and yet,
To-morrow is not to be found.

Whose shadow crosses every sea
To lands the Empire found and made;
The stranger bends in awe, while we,
Thy children prosper in its shade.

Thy mirage is a bulwark spread
By bush, and plain, and veldt, and strand;
You vigil in the abstract — guard
And master where you do not stand.

Whose watch includes all cast and cult —
A duty greater than we know;
Unprecedented since you keep
The peace while struggling with a foe.

The greatest Empire yet evolved
Speaks from thy many throated decks;
In battle stern as master mild —
While conquering you inspire respects.

The fleet! the fleet! the British fleet
Which vigils in the storm and lull;
Protects our ancient rights and makes
The British Empire possible!

IT MAKES ME MAD

It makes me mad
To think that through my life-time I have had
Sufficient wealth to choke a city sewer,
Yet I am poor.

It has me beaten
To think that through my life-time I have eaten
Sufficient food to fill a giant bin,
Yet I am thin.

It makes me wild
To think that through my life I have beguiled
In study many hours at great expense,
Yet I am dense.

It tires my head
To think that through my life-time I have read
Sufficient books to fill a railroad car,
Yet more there are.

It "gets my goat"
To think that through my life-time I have "wrote"
Sufficient books to make a nation groan,
Yet am unknown.

Yet I am glad,
For though I'm poor, and wild, and dense, and mad,
And yet unknown, with each attending curse,
I might be worse.

THE DIPLOMAT

I have to be a diplomat at everything I do —
A diplomat at everything I say;
For I may step on some great person's highly
      polished shoe,
Or get myself in other people's way.

I have to be a diplomat at everything I get —
I must be diplomatic when I buy;
For I may need the dollars when my days get cold
      and wet —
I must live low while living is so high.

I have to be a diplomat at everything I write —
A diplomat at reading of the news;
For I may touch the "touchy" in the passion of my
      flight;
I may get narrow-minded in my views.

I have to be a diplomat at everything I hear —
A diplomat at everything I see;
And I must sift them in at one and out the other
      ear —
They may be colored to environ me.

I have to be a diplomat at everything I sign —
I must be diplomatic when I tell;
For I may write away from me the birth-claims that
      are mine,
My words may be of value and may sell.

If I am not a diplomat at everything I prize —
Were I not blessed with diplomatic trends,
I might be made a stepping-stone to elevate the
      wise,
Or used to further other people's ends.

*Two poems from CHIPS OFF THE OLD BLOCK by Lew Cummings**

JUST A WORN OUT DAD

Getting blind in one eye,
The other's just as bad;
My knees are stiff and wabbly,
I'm just a worn out dad.

What hair I've left is greyish,
Wrinkles make me sad;
My pants need another pressing,
I'm just a worn out dad.

Manners are abrupt and shameful,
No pep as when a lad,
Seem happy the way I'm living,
I'm just a worn out dad.

Kids don't heed my warning,
When doing a modern fad,
They think I'm old and foolish,
And just a worn out dad.

Don't care 'bout spending money,
Wish I kept every cent I had,
Getting to be a miser,
I'm just a worn out dad.

Can't see no fun in nothing,
Grouchy and seldom glad,
Everything seems to worry me,
I'm just a worn out dad.

THE GRANDEST SORT OF GUY

There is a man in our town,
The grandest sort of guy,
Whose patience is amazing,
With things he wants to try.

He smiles to all who pass him,
In a sort of warm hello.
He never kicks or grouches,
And is always on the go.

He's always ever willing
When it comes to doing things,
And like the George who does it
Results he always brings

He never sings or whistles,
But mildly in his way,
His life is full of goodness
And deeds he does each day.

He's a little bit old fashioned,
His manners always right,
But when he's ruffled slightly,
He never wants to fight.

There is a man in our town,
He's the grandest sort of guy —
He's only past six months,
And that's the reason why.

A Note on Sources

The articles in this book were all made possible by the fine collection of information about local history that has been assembled over the years at the Ashcroft Museum and Archives. Also useful were Bruce Hutchinson's *The Fraser* (Toronto: Irwin, 1950), Art Downs' *Wagon Road North* (Surrey, BC: Heritage House, 1993); Margaret Ormsby's classic *British Columbia: A History* (Toronto: Macmillan, 1958); Jessie Ann Smith's *Widow Smith of Spence's Bridge* (Merritt, BC: Sonotek, 1989); and Helen Forster's article "From Transport to Tomatoes" in Wayne Norton and Wilf Schmidt's *Reflections: Thompson Valley Histories* (Kamloops, BC: Plateau Press, 1994).

Motorists at the Ashcroft Hotel (BCARS D-09299)

Historic Ashcroft

When noted Canadian journalist Bruce Hutchinson wrote about his visit to the Ashcroft area in the 1950s, he said the scenery was "for the strong eye only." His opinion was that the harshness of the landscape could please but few observers.

With this new collection of historic articles and photographs, Pat Foster proudly steps forward as one of the few. Arguing that both the landscape and the local past deserve greater recognition, Foster offers the reader essays on selected topics of Ashcroft's history that have captured her attention. From the great fire of 1916 to the freighters of the BX Company, from the Chinese community to the annals of the historic *Ashcroft Journal*, Pat Foster demonstrates that the people of Ashcroft have shared a unique history.

Offered in this limited edition, *For the Strong Eye Only* is the work of an author who would like nothing more than to share with her readers the treasure she has discovered in Ashcroft history.

Plateau Press / 72 pages / $13.95
Ashcroft/Thompson Valley History

ISBN 0-9698842-3-0

9 780969 884231